Spirit-Led Prayers Get Results

When PRAYER is a PRIORITY,
VICTORY is INEVITABLE!

KAREN JETHROE

SPIRIT-LED PRAYERS GET RESULTS
When prayer is a priority, victory is inevitable!

Scripture verses marked NLT are taken from the NEW LIVING TRANSLATION. Scripture verses marked AMP are taken from the AMPLIFIED BIBLE. Scripture verses marked KJV are taken from the KING JAMES VERSION of the BIBLE. Scripture verses marked MSG are taken from THE MESSAGE TRANSLATION. Scripture verses marked CEV are taken from the CONTEMPORARY ENGLISH TRANSLATION. Scripture verses marked NKJV are taken from the NEW KING JAMES VERSION of the BIBLE.

ISBN 13: 978-0692795507
Religion/Christian Life/Prayer
Printed in the United States of America

Dedication

Dear brothers and sisters, honor those who are your leaders in the Lord's work. They work hard among you and give you spiritual guidance.
(1 Thessalonians 5:12 NLT)

I dedicate this book to my pastor, friend, and spiritual covering, Pastor Frederick D. Nettles (Living Word Fellowship). You have been faithful to pray me out of my problems and push me into my potential and purpose. You changed the way I saw myself as a woman who has been called to lead. If it were not for your counsel and encouragement, I would have quit. I will forever be grateful to you and your lovely wife Wanda.

To Pastor Rose Lusk (New Beginnings OutReach Ministries), your faithfulness in praying for me and my family leaves me speechless. I am so grateful to you. You have taught me that when prayer is the priority, God will move in one's favor.

To Kim Potter (A New Thing Ministries), your talk and your walk are seamless. It is such an honor for me to call you my trusted friend. Your writings have ministered to me more times than I can count. Oftentimes, it's as if you were writing to me only. Thank you so much for the calls, the listening ear, the honesty, the laughs, and the prayers. Truly you are a General in God's Kingdom.

Acknowledgements

To my Lord and Savior, Jesus Christ! As cliché as it may sound, without you I can do nothing. Thank you for my life, my gift, my journey.

To my parents, Stanley (R.I.P.) and Barbara Caldron, thank you for having me and for training me up in the way that I should go. I have never departed from it.

To my husband and children, nothing in life has taught me the power of prayer as much as my life with you. Thank you for accepting God's call on my life even when you did not understand it.

To my siblings, Renee and Gina, thank you for showing me the epitome of sacrificial love.

To my eleven grandchildren, my niece and nephew, thank you for constantly reminding me that I am loved and appreciated.

To my personal assistant, Dionne, thank you for your patience, endurance, and faith to stick it out with me.

Finally, to KINGDOM LIFE CHRISTIAN MINISTRIES, not only are you my godly assignment but you are my joy! Thank you for taking this journey with me.

Table of Contents

Introduction

If I can be honest with you, there have been times when I have found it hard to believe what is written in some passages of Scripture. Well, maybe saying that it was hard for me to believe is a little too harsh. After all, I would never want to imply in any way that the Writer, the Interpreter, the Revealer of God's heart and mind, (Holy Spirit) got it wrong. No, He is the Spirit of Truth and I know the onus is not on him. I take all responsibility for my lack of faith. I take responsibility for my lack of building a genuine consistent relationship with Holy Spirit. If I had done that in my early years, believing every word in Scripture would have been so much easier for me.

What I am trying to say is that there have been times when it was hard for me to believe that every passage written included me. I know better now. In one way or another, *all* the messages recorded in God's Holy Bible are profitable for me (2 Timothy 3:16). Unfortunately, in the religious environment that I came from, it was much easier for me to believe and to accept that all the consequences of sin were immediately mine, but not so when it came to the promises found in the same Book. Over time, this deeply affected my prayer life. Prayer became more like work without ever knowing if I would or would not receive a fair wage on pay day. How badly I needed a prayer answered would determine the length and the fervency of my prayer. I would even include fasting when I thought it would get the job done quicker or that it would deliver, with complete accuracy, everything that I had prayed for.

Now I know some of you reading this may think I was manipulating God. This was not the case at all. I was praying from a very sincere heart, practicing what I had been taught and what I had seen demonstrated to me. There were other times when my prayers were just rote patterns of speech with little or no faith attached to them. This prayer journey of mine has often left me standing merciless with a stifled tongue and liquid prayers before the only One who held the answers to all of my problems. I was very much like Hannah (1 Samuel 1:10-15) when she was praying for a son. At some point, words failed her and she wept bitterly. When Eli thought she was drunk, she defended herself with these words, *"Oh no, sir!" she replied. "I haven't been drinking wine or anything stronger. But I am very discouraged, and I was pouring out my heart to the LORD."*

Have you ever been there? Do you have a history of hit and miss answers to prayer? How has it affected your faith? What has it done to your consistency in prayer? How often have you been discouraged while in the process of praying?

8

I know these are tough questions, but they need to be asked and they need to be answered - honestly. I remember one of the things missing from my early church experience is that not many people told their entire story. I don't know if they were trying to protect their image or God's. In either case, they were not thorough and left out parts that were critical to my prayer walk, as well as my faith walk.

My goal is to be as transparent as Holy Spirit allows me to be. I want to expose the machinations of an enemy who once kept me guilt-ridden over prayers that were never answered and discouraged over the ones that I was still holding on for. I don't promise to know all the answers, but I promise to give you all the ones that I do know that helped me to develop a Spirit-led prayer life that consistently gets results in line with the will of God for my life.

Chapter 1

It's Really Not That Hard

Therefore I say unto you, What things soever ye desire,
when ye pray, believe that ye receive them,
and ye shall have them.
(Mark 11:24 KJV)

All of us are benefactors of prayer. If you are born again, I can tell you that prayer initiated that experience. Someone prayed you into the Kingdom of God. God placed you on somebody's heart and they prayed for your salvation, whether they knew you or not. Through their prayers, God began the process of calling you to Him by his Holy Spirit. John 6:44 says, *"No one can come to Me unless the Father who sent Me draws him; and I will raise him up at the last day."* When you responded to the "draw" of the Holy Spirit and accepted Jesus as your Savior, you did so with a prayer:

"...that if you confess with your mouth the Lord Jesus
and believe in your heart that God has raised Him from
the dead, you will be saved. For with the heart one believes

unto righteousness, and with the mouth confession is made unto salvation."
(Romans 10:9-10)

The evidence that God heard your prayer was the result of you being saved. You believed what you prayed for and you got results. You got what you expected. It's just that easy!

I believe prayer is the alpha and omega of a victorious life in Christ Jesus. Most people I have come in contact with who feel sluggish in their Christian walk are those who are sluggish in their prayer lives. Prayer is what adds vitality to this walk, and the results we get from it is what motivates us to continue in prayer. James 5:16 teaches us that it's the *fervent* prayers which get results.

But some of you may say that it is the lack of *results* that have caused you to stop praying or to be inconsistent about it. I understand that, because I was once there. I prayed for many things that I did not get. It became very discouraging and I began to feel like a spiritual dunce. I could hear the enemy snickering and taunting me with Mark 11:24: *"Therefore I say unto you, What things soever ye desire, when ye pray, believe that ye receive them, and ye shall have them."* I knew God answered prayer, because prayers were answered all around me. It made me ask myself what was I doing wrong and what was I going to do about it? Like a child learning to ride a bike without training wheels, would I give up and just watch others enjoy riding their two-wheelers, or would I continue my quest to seek and receive answers to my prayers?

One thing I have learned about prayer is that you must keep it "Father-focused." When Jesus was teaching his disciples to pray, he told them to pray like this: *Our Father...* (Matthew 6:9). I believe Jesus was letting them know the secret to answered prayers is directly related to our relationship with the Father, just as it was for him. He makes this clear in John 6:30, *"I can of mine own self do nothing; as I hear, I judge; and my judgment is just; because I seek not mine own will, but the will of the Father which has sent me."*

As many times as I have read this passage of scripture, one day it spoke to me in a different way. What an eye-opening moment that was for me! Holy Spirit was teaching me something about the way I should be praying as opposed to the way I had been praying. I was about to experience a breakthrough in understanding Mark 11:24.

I began to understand that prayers which get results are the ones birthed from a relationship with the Father. Just like Jesus, I came from the Father. It is the will of the Father that I am in the earth and I am here to accomplish His will and not my own will, as had been the way I always prayed. But it was also the only way I knew to pray, because even though I came from the Father, I did not know the Father. Unlike Jesus, I could not say that I knew His voice, much less His will. To make matters worse, I didn't know myself either. I thought I did, and I would pray according to what I thought I knew about myself. Let me tell you, I have learned to thank God for all the prayers that He did not answer!

This new revelation coerced me to go back to square one in my prayer life. I realized that prayer was not just about getting things done or getting things, for that matter. Prayer was about getting to know the Father first and foremost. This did not start off easy for me. I had so much "unlearning" to do. I had to break some bad habits, like always talking first instead of listening. I had to learn how to just sit in silence and to be okay with that. I had to learn how to wait on Holy Spirit to pray through me or to tell me what to pray. Romans 8:26-27 (NLT) was my go-to scripture to help me during this transition:

> *And the Holy Spirit helps us in our weakness. For example, we don't know what God wants us to pray for. But the Holy Spirit prays for us with groanings that cannot be expressed in words. And the Father who knows all hearts knows what the Spirit is saying, for the Spirit pleads for us believers in harmony with God's own will.*

During this time, I began to fall in love with the Father. All of His attributes were appealing to me. The abundance of love, mercy, grace and truth flowed freely from Him to me. I began to crave time alone with Him just to bathe in His presence. I would ask for nothing and yet I would leave full and complete. I was learning Him and I was learning me. And what was more amazing was that there were things about me I knew He didn't like, but He still longed to be with me.

This revelation literally changed everything about my prayer life and, ultimately, it changed me. The more I grew in my relationship with the Father, the more He revealed His heart to me. And in the heart of the Father, I began to see what His desires were for me. Jeremiah 29:11 (NIV) says it best, *"For I know the plans I have for you,' declares the Lord, 'plans to prosper you and not to harm you, plans to give you hope and a future."*

I got it! It was clear to me why so many of my prayers had gone unanswered. They did not line up with the plans that the Father had for my life. Then, I didn't know the Father's heart and what his desires were for me, but I'm grateful I do now. I now know how to pray and let Holy Spirit pray through me. I know to spend time with the Father and to allow the Holy Spirit to reveal God's heart to me. The more He shows me, the more I accurately incorporate Mark 11:24 into my prayer life to get the results that line up with His desire for me: *"Therefore I say unto you, What things soever ye desire, when ye pray, believe that ye receive them, and ye shall have them."* Spirit-led prayers really do get results!

Chapter 2

Love is the Key

"And we have known and believed the love that God has for us.
God is love, and he who abides in love abides in God,
and God in him.
(1 John 4:16)

If I asked you if you really believe that God loves you, what would you say? Some of you would say yes and your answer would be correct. It is certainly the answer I always gave, but when it came to my unanswered prayers, it is not the answer I always believed. The bible says that God loves everybody, yet the enemy would remind me that God did not love me "as much" as He loved the ones whose prayers were answered. When I began to believe this lie, it made me question if God even loved me at all. I knew the scripture in John 3:16, *"For God so loved the world that He gave His only begotten Son, that whoever believes in Him should not perish but have everlasting life."* I believed this scripture for my salvation, but it meant nothing to me in regards to why God was not answering my prayers. This was more personal to me. Once again, instead of my prayer life being all about God, it was all about me.

It took me a while to pinpoint where my erroneous perception about God and His lack of love for me came from. I was blessed with a very loving dad who was gentle and served God as far back as I can remember. My dad was always forgiving and believed the best in me and for me. When I would mess up or get out of line, he would correct me, but he would not stay angry with me. At any given moment, I could run back into his loving arms knowing that nothing had changed the way he felt about me or the way I felt about him. If anything, I loved him more and more with each experience.

I know some have said our relationship with God, the Father, will resemble whatever relationship we have with our earthly father. But this was not true for me at this point in my journey. I clearly remember relating to God as God, and not as Father. To me, He was God the judge. He was God the chastiser. He was the God who kept score. He was God who forgave but did not forget. He was the God who loved the saints that never messed up, tolerated the ones who did, and hated sinners altogether. Sadly, this perception caused me to treat others the way I thought God treated me, and I believed this was being holy because God is holy.

In hindsight, it is little wonder why answers to my prayers were hindered. I did not know the love of God. I did not know the loving God in a personal way. I knew the rules of the church. I knew the doctrine of man. I had what is referred to as "head" knowledge of scripture with no revelation from Holy Spirit. Even though I was faithful to working in the house of God and an ardent student of scripture, rarely did the word of God find good ground in my heart, and the lack of good fruit (answered prayers) proved it. I was miserable, frustrated, confused, and I didn't know what to do about it.

It took a series of events involving my adult children that helped me to understand the kind of love God has for me. It may sound like a strange thing to say, but I think I learned to love my children the right way from the sinful things they did as adults more so than when they were children. When they were children they had to submit to my authority. They had to exhibit godly behavior on the outside, even if it was not who they truly were. It was important that they obeyed me and made me look good. When they stepped out of line, I would correct them harshly in whatever way I thought would get the results I wanted or, better yet, needed. During that time, I would use the word of God to justify my actions. Proverbs 22:15 was all the ammunition I needed to bring my children in line:

Foolishness is bound up in the heart of a child; The rod of correction will drive it far from him.

Even though I was using the rod as an act of love, the force of anger that guided the rod certainly did not come across as a loving act. To this day, my oldest child believed his mother was just crazy!

As my children became adults and were guided less and less by my influence, they began to reveal what I thought my strict disciplinary actions had removed from them. They began to walk in sinful patterns they never saw demonstrated in the home where they were raised. Romans 5:8 states, *"But God demonstrates His own love toward us, in that while we were still sinners, Christ died for us."* This passage of scripture became the catalyst that led to the beginning of the salvation of my soul. I didn't say the salvation of my spirit man. My spirit man was saved the instant I gave my heart to Jesus. Soul salvation is a process.

The soul is the place where the mind, will, intellect, emotions, passions, lusts, etc., reside and operate. The Apostle Paul describes it in Romans 8:6-7,

For to be carnally minded is death; but to be spiritually minded is life and peace. Because the carnal mind is enmity against God: for it is not subject to the law of God, neither indeed can be.

When you are carnally minded, you can best be described as a "dead head." There is no life of the spirit flowing from you. You are saved, but you have no peace and no rest. The carnal mind is in constant animosity against God. The carnal mind feeds and pleases the flesh, while the spirit man is yearning to please God. This is total anarchy (*a state of total disorder due to absence or non-recognition of authority*).

18

My saved and sanctified image was being exposed for the mess it really was. It seemed the more I prayed for my children, the worst they got. I now realize that because I was praying carnal-minded prayers, I did not get the results I desired despite all my fasting and praying. My prayers for their deliverance had more to do with my image, my comfort, my peace, and little to do with their true deliverance. It had nothing to do with the way God felt about them. My eyes were blinded by my own self-righteousness because my heart was bound to my religious rules of conduct.

I remember being taught to pray prayers for our unsaved loved ones in a way that would release the wrath of God on them, rather than the love of God. These prayers in no way resembled Romans 2:4 (NLT):

Don't you see how wonderfully kind, tolerant, and patient God is with you? Does this mean nothing to you? ***Can't you see that his kindness is intended to turn you from your sin?***

God's kindness was intended to turn us from sin, not the wrath that I was giving Him permission to unleash on those that refused to bend to the well-constructed, fire infused, scripturally supported, loveless prayers that I passionately prayed from my carnal mind. In hindsight, I really did think I was praying the right prayers for the right reasons. I genuinely love my family and wanted to see all my loved ones saved. I honestly thought I was telling them the truth.

What I did not know then but now understand, is that love without truth is false and truth without love is harsh.

As the scales began to fall off of my eyes, I had to re-evaluate my own salvation. Did I become born again out of fear of destruction, or was it because I sincerely believed that God loved me? Did I sincerely believe that I would have a happier life and be a better person if I allowed Jesus to come and live in my heart? Or did I become born again for the one purpose of avoiding hell? Finally, had my experience lived up to the expectation? Let me begin by answering the first question. Yes, my reasons for accepting Jesus into my life were right and real. I remember, even at 16 years of age, being a miserable sinner. I remember feeling a void of love in my life that nothing and nobody could fill. I had two very loving parents, grandparents and great-grandparents. I had two loving sisters, and I had good friends in my life as well. Truthfully, in those relationships I could have easily be named as the unloving one. I hated church, and frequently and unlovingly let it be shown through my behavior. I openly refused many opportunities for salvation before I eventually said yes. I think it was because I knew that there was something very real about serving God and I did not want to commit out of politeness to the preacher. I wanted to be real when the right time came and it did come. It came when I did not expect it. It came where I did not expect it. It came when I had other plans to continue in my sins and to expand my desperate, selfish search for love to fill this void in my heart. I don't know how many people can remember the details of when they became born again, but I can. I can remember the year and the month. I remember the name of the church and the city it was in. I remember the speaker and the title of the sermon. And what I remember best of all is the love of God that drew me to that altar to surrender my heart to him. I remember tears falling and burdens being lifted. I remember realizing that this was a decision I would never regret, and one that would change the course of my life.

Never once did I think about avoiding hell as much as I thought about entering into a relationship with Jesus Christ. The year was 1969 and, to this day, I have never regretted making that decision. I penned a poem to describe my experience from *2 Corinthians 5:17 (NKJV): "Therefore, if anyone is in Christ, he is a new creation; old things have passed away; behold, all things have become new."*

I came to Him so torn and ragged with little hope at all.
He stood before me, arms outstretched and I yielded to His call.
So many had hurt me times before and yet it seemed like I
Just had to give to Him the chance to prove He wasn't a lie.
I didn't search His background and hoped for me the same.
For my past had been so ugly and filled with great shame,

*That I knew it would be easier for Him to be my
friend,*
*If I could only keep from Him my terrible life of
sin.*
*But as I stood before Him those things I'd hoped to
hide*
*All flashed before Him yet he did not seem
surprised.*
*Repentant tears began to fall and somehow it all
seemed true.*
*To him my past was in the past and we started life
anew.*

This leads me to answer the last question, of whether my experience lived up to my expectations? Initially, I said no, but not for the reasons some may think. I was not an unhappy Christian. How could I be? I was in the right church, getting the right teaching from the right people. I was trying to do all the right things, even when I was getting the wrong results. You see, I wasn't unhappy. I was unfulfilled. I didn't know how to grow in the love that drew me to God in the first place. I spent so many years fasting, praying, consecrating, repenting, judging, condemning, trying to please God and trying to get God to love me like I loved him. I spent countless hours working in the church for him. I would present my "works" before him proudly. If there was a crown in heaven for those who were faithful to "works," I surely had earned mine many times over. I was doing everything for God, but I was doing nothing with

God. I became addicted to the work of the church and like every addict, I kept chasing that first high. I wanted to feel that same love that drew me to the Father in the first place. What I failed to realize at the time is that I was looking for it in the wrong places:

For by grace you have been saved through faith, and that not of yourselves; it is the gift of God, not of works, lest anyone should boast.
(Ephesians 2:8-9 NKJV)

That kind of love did not come from church work; it came from being in the presence of the Father. It came from needing Him more than anything else. I had left my first love without even knowing it.

Chapter 3

The Process

And no one puts new wine into old wineskins. For the old skins would burst from the pressure, spilling the wine and ruining the skins. New wine is stored in new wineskins so that both are preserved.
(Matthew 9:17 NLT)

Even with my new revelation, I did not leave my church immediately. I loved my church family, I respected the leadership and, honestly, I never thought there would be an issue. However, over time the rules got to be too much for me to bear. Holy Spirit was beginning to bring me into truth that had been hidden from me due to my lack of relationship with the Father and lack of relationship with His word. When I made a decision to study the word of the Lord beyond Sunday school, Sunday morning service, and weekly bible study, Holy Spirit joined me. He began to open my eyes as the truth of the word began to shed light in the dark areas of my mind and my heart. I began to experience Psalm 119:130 – *"The entrance of Your words give light; it gives understanding to the simple."*

As I studied God's word and increased my prayer life, I began to break free from the religious bondage that had held me captive since the day of my salvation. This liberty was amazing, but I did not know how to handle it properly. I was still in a church that adhered to religious rules and I would flaunt my liberty in front of them. I was trying to pour my new wine (revelation) into old wineskins...without permission. I remember one day while at church, Holy Spirit rebuked me. He told me that as long as I remained at that church that I had to respect the leadership, or I could leave. Needless to say, I left. It was the hardest but best decision I could have made, because it led me to a whole new experience in my Christian walk. I was about to learn how to live a Spirit-filled, Spirit-led life. I would learn it through the development of the fruit of the Spirit in the everyday circumstances of life.

In the fifth chapter of Galatians, there is a clear description given between the fruit of the Spirit and the works of the flesh. Our flesh has desires and there is only one way not to give in to them.

But I say, may you walk in the spirit so that you would not in any way fulfil any desire of the flesh. For the flesh turns against the spirit, and the spirit against the flesh, these things are opposed to one another, so that you would not do the things you want to do."
(Galatians 5:16-17 ONM)

25

Prior to the process of pruning, I had read Galatians 5:19-21 many times, but only from the perspective of how it related to the sinner. Let's look at these verses:

When you follow the desires of your sinful nature, your lives will produce these evil results: sexual immorality, impure thoughts, eagerness for lustful pleasure, idolatry, participation in demonic activities, hostility, quarreling, jealousy, outbursts of anger, selfish ambition, divisions, the feeling that everyone is wrong except those in your own little group, envy, drunkenness, wild parties, and other kinds of sin. Let me tell you again, as I have before, that anyone living that sort of life will not inherit the Kingdom of God.

It was not until I became a true student in the *School of The Holy Spirit* that I began to see myself in the mirror of the Word of God. Even though verse 18 stated that I was no longer under the law of the flesh if I was Spirit led, verses 19-21 revealed some things that were still present in my life. Of course, I was blind to them because my focus was on the ones that I was sure did not fit my spiritual profile. I wasn't immoral or a drunkard; neither was I impure. However, out of the more than 15 sins listed, at least five of them were very active in my life. How could this be? And I am sure if I had looked up the definitions of some of the words I did not know at the time, the list could have been longer. Not only were some things present in my Christian life that should not have been, there were also things absent that should have been present.

> *But when the Holy Spirit controls our lives, he will produce this kind of fruit in us: love, joy, peace, patience, kindness, goodness, faithfulness, gentleness, and self-control. Here there is no conflict with the law.*
> (Galatians 5:22-23 NLT)

Once again, it became clear to me why many of my prayers were hitting a brick wall. Many of my prayers came from a place of selfish ambition, jealousy, envy and anger. There was no love, I had no patience, and there was nothing kind about the way I felt when God did not answer my prayers. In retrospect, I was a "hot mess" and I really needed help. Little did I know of the painful, pruning process that it was going to take to get me to the place where I would sincerely believe Philippians 1:6 to be true about me: *"God, who began the good work within you, will continue his work until it is finally finished on that day when Christ Jesus comes back again."*

Let me tell you, when I positioned myself properly in the process, I was able to endure the pruning. When it was revealed to me that if I let the Holy Spirit control my life then He would produce the fruit of the Spirit in me, I stopped trying to do it on my own. When it was revealed to me that it was God who began this work in my life and it would take God to complete it, I stopped trying to do it on my own. My flesh was no longer the boss of me. I began to make room for Holy Spirit to lead and guide me in all of my ways, beginning with my prayer life.

One passage of scripture that really spoke to me during the process was John 15:1-2, *"I am the true vine, and my Father is the gardener. He cuts off every branch that doesn't produce fruit, and he prunes the branches that do bear fruit so they will produce even more."*

The first thing Holy Spirit revealed to me in this text was that when we pray, we are to produce results. When we don't, then something is wrong. We know that it is God who answers our prayers, but He cannot answer prayers that are not in line with His will. So the process for me began with cutting some things totally out of my life. This was something that I had to do on my own. This was a choice that I had to make. It meant that there were people that I had to sever ties with. They were people who were toxic to my growth in Christ, those who had too much of a carnal influence in my life, and those whose season was over in my life. I also had to sever my relationship with carnal things. Anything that was enmity to God had to be cut off and done away with for good. This was necessary so that when I prayed, my prayers would not have to be filtered through mounds of carnal attachments.

Secondly, there were some areas of my life that were producing fruit. As I said before, some of my prayers were getting answered. However, I was expected to bear more fruit. I was weak in some areas of faith, which also plays a part in our prayers being answered. In Matthew 9:27-29, two blind men approach Jesus and beg for healing. They believed Jesus could heal them and he did. He said to them in verse 29, *"Then He touched their eyes, saying, 'According to your faith let it be to you."*

In this text, Holy Spirit revealed to me that another reason why some of my prayers were not being answered was because I didn't have the faith to even pray them. This is where the discipline (pruning) of the Holy Spirit began to show up vigorously in my life. This was the boot camp of all boot camps in getting to know Him. I remember the day he said to me, "You and Me, the new we!" It was a setup I never saw coming. I was so excited over those words. Holy Spirit and I were about to be tight! I thought I was something really special, until friends became inaccessible, funds began to shrink, ministering began to feel like a chore, and my flesh was suffering. He was pruning me. He was teaching me; He was delivering me; and He was keeping me. During this season, my faith grew by leaps and bounds, because as He was teaching me to pray the will of the Father, He would have me to pray some of the most outlandish prayers. Some might say that they were unbelievable, and it would be true as it relates to the carnal mind, but that is where the pruning process was taking place...in my carnal mind.

Praying in faith became easier and more natural for me as I began to fill my mind with the Word of God.

So then faith comes by hearing, and hearing by the word of God.
(Romans 10:17)

This discipline of the Holy Spirit would unction me to continuously study the Word of God. This meant that it was my responsibility to make it a priority and to set aside time specifically to renew my mind with the Word of God as instructed in Romans 12:2, *"And do not be conformed to this world, but be transformed by the renewing of your mind, that you may prove what is that good and acceptable and perfect will of God."*

Holy Spirit was teaching me that the only way to pray spirit-led prayers was to know the mind of God. The only way to know the mind of God was to read what God has spoken. His will is in His Word!!

Chapter 4

What's In a Name?

*"You can ask for anything in my name, and I will
do it, because the work of the Son brings
glory to the Father.
Yes, ask anything in my name, and I will do it!"*
(John 14:13-14 NLT)

If you are familiar with your bible, then you know that no one comes to the Father except through Jesus (John 14:6). He is our Savior and He is our intercessor, or the one who mediates for us according to Hebrews 7:26, *"Therefore He is also able to save to the uttermost those who come to God through Him, since He always lives to make intercession for them."*

Jesus is the one who makes it possible for us to get our prayers answered, because He gives us the authority to use his name. This is a name that has great influence in every realm, according to Philippians 2:9-10 KJV, *"Wherefore God also hath highly exalted him, and given him a name which is above every name: That at the name of Jesus every knee should bow, of things in heaven, and things in earth, and things under the earth."*

31

This is a name that we have the authority to use. This is great news for the believer. It is a reminder that the enemy has no power over us when we use the name of Jesus.

Think about the influence that this name carries. Influence is *the power to change or affect someone or something: the power to cause changes without directly forcing them to happen.* I love this definition because it talks about the power to change things. That's what Spirit-led praying is all about. How do you know when a prayer is answered? When you see that something has changed! That's when you know that your prayers were effective. Let's take a look at James 5:16 (NLT):

Confess your sins to each other and pray for each other so that you may be healed. The earnest prayer of a righteous person has great power and produces wonderful results."

There is no doubt that Spirit-led prayers will bring about change.

Let's look at some of the ways that using the name of Jesus brings change. In Acts Chapter 3, we read where Peter and John went up to the temple at the time of prayer. Just as they were going in, there was a man who was lame from birth and daily he would be carried and laid at the gate of the Temple, begging for alms from those who were entering the Temple. But this day, he received more than what he was begging for and more than he expected. He got something that would change his life and his way of living:

32

Peter and John looked at him intently, and Peter said, "Look at us!" The lame man looked at them eagerly, expecting some money. But Peter said, "I don't have any silver or gold for you. But I'll give you what I have. In the name of Jesus Christ the Nazarene, get up and walk!" Then Peter took the lame man by the right hand and helped him up. And as he did, the man's feet and ankles were instantly healed and strengthened. He jumped up, stood on his feet, and began to walk! Then, walking, leaping, and praising God, he went into the Temple with them."

That's what the name of Jesus does; it brings change. If you have some situations in your life that money, nor anything else can fix, then try speaking to those situations using the name of Jesus, and watch what happens. You and I have been given the authority to use His name to bring about Kingdom influence everywhere we go. This name will bring you into a new realm of life. The lame man, from his mother's womb, was only familiar with an environment that required help. He had never lived beyond what others provided for him. He would never reach beyond what those handouts provided him. He lacked all ability to do for himself and he never expected anything to change. Can you imagine just how amazed he was to be healed? I don't know if he had ever heard of anyone being healed or if he had ever seen it. I don't know if he thought healing only happened in the Temple and, therefore, it would never happen for him.

All I know, is that at the name of Jesus, his life changed forever and he did not keep it to himself:

He jumped up, stood on his feet, and began to walk! Then, walking, leaping, and praising God, he went into the Temple with them.

Just look at the immediate progress in his life. He went from walking, to leaping, to praising (which I imagine is dancing) all in the same day! The name of Jesus has great influence in heaven and when we pray we can expect good results.

In another scenario, the disciples fully understood the power of Spirit-led prayers and the influence that the name of Jesus had with his Father. In Acts Chapter 4, their desire was that all followers of the gospel of Jesus Christ would have boldness in spite of every threat for their lives. They needed courage to do the things that they were commanded to do in carrying out the gospel. This desire prompted them to pray for proof that would undeniably convince others that the name of Jesus is powerful when used. They prayed to God, " *Stretch out your hand with healing power; may miraculous signs and wonders be done through the name of your holy servant Jesus"* (Acts 4:30).

I am sure most of you reading this book can identify with how they must have been feeling. Jesus had been taken up at this point. He had told them that they shall do greater works than he had done and that he was sending back the Holy Spirit to dwell in them and to give them power to carry out their assignment. Look at how once again Spirit-led prayers brought about change in the next verse: *"After this prayer, the meeting place shook, and they were all filled with the Holy Spirit. Then they preached the word of God with boldness."*

The name of Jesus has influence in the Kingdom of God to bring about manifested change in the earth, but that is not the only place it has influence. Let's look at Acts 16:16-18:

> *Now it happened, as we went to prayer, that a certain slave girl possessed with a spirit of divination met us, who brought her masters much profit by fortune-telling. This girl followed Paul and us, and cried out, saying, 'These men are the servants of the Most High God, who proclaim to us the way of salvation.' And this she did for many days. But Paul, greatly annoyed, turned and said to the spirit, 'I command you in the name of Jesus Christ to come out of her." And he came out that very hour.*

The name of Jesus has influence in the kingdom of darkness to the point of bringing about visible change in the earth. The name of Jesus has authority in every dimension! The evil spirit in this woman had no controlling power over the name of Jesus. He controlled the woman and he attempted to control Paul's environment. Have you ever had to deal with an annoying spirit that was messing with your spiritual flow? And how often does it show up when you are about to enter into prayer? You do not have to put up with it. You can do as Paul did and speak to the evil spirit and command it to go in the name of Jesus, and it will flee immediately.

We have been commanded in scripture to do all things in the name of Jesus (Colossians 3:17). What does that look like for the Body of Christ? The Apostle Paul makes it pretty clear in 1 Corinthians 1:10 (NASB), *"Now I exhort you, brethren, by the name of our Lord Jesus Christ, that you all agree and that there be no divisions among you, but that you be made complete in the same mind and in the same judgment."* Did you know that there is enough power in the name of Jesus to cause the Body of Christ to walk in agreement? Yes, in the name of Jesus you can command the spirit of division, racism, jealousy, backbiting, strife, etc., to flee. The power and authority that is in the name of Jesus is the power to love the unlovable, to bring peace in the most chaotic situations, and to find a place of agreement for the sake of the Kingdom. The enemy knows that if he can keep the Body of Christ divided that we diminish greatly in our power against him. But when we are yielded to the Holy Spirit and we allow him to direct our prayers, we will pray prayers that bring about change. We will pray prayers that are in line with the will of God, even when our natural minds do not comprehend it or agree with it.

Are you willing to use the name of Jesus to influence your personal mindset and the way that you see things that are not in line with God's word? Are you willing to embrace unity in the Body of Christ when it means you have to admit that you were wrong about some things and are you ready to apologize? What did the Apostle Paul say he was willing to do for the name of Jesus?

> Then Paul replied, "What are you doing, weeping and
> breaking my heart [like this]? For I am ready not only to
> be bound and imprisoned, but even to die at Jerusalem for
> the name of the Lord Jesus."
> (Acts 21:13 AMP)

What an influence the name of Jesus had on his life! What change was brought about in his life as he committed and sacrificed himself to spreading the gospel! The Apostle Paul was aware that there would be no victories apart from a spirit-filled life and a spirit-led prayer life. He knew that there were spiritual strategies that had to be put in place and adhered to. In Ephesians 6:11-17, he enlightens us to the spiritual warfare that we are engaged in and he instructs us to put on the whole armor of God. He describes the amour in detail so that we will know that we are well-protected. What I love most is what Paul says in verse 18 (AMP), *"With all prayer and petition pray [with specific requests] at all times [on every occasion and in every season] in the Spirit, and with this in view, stay alert with all perseverance and petition [interceding in prayer] for all God's people."*

The Apostle Paul admonishes us to pray in the Spirit! It doesn't matter how well-suited up you may be for the battle, if you are not praying Spirit-led prayers, you will not win. Unless the Spirit directs your prayers, you won't know what weapon to use for the battle that you are engaging in.

Unless the Spirit directs your prayers, you won't know what scripture to use for the battle that you are engaging in. Unless the Spirit directs your prayers, you will forget the authority that you have to use the name of Jesus. Spirit-led prayers get results!

Chapter 5

Lord, Teach Us to Pray

Our Father in heaven,
Hallowed be Your name.
Your kingdom come.
Your will be done
On earth as it is in heaven.
(Luke 11:2)

In Luke 11, the disciples asked Jesus to teach them how to pray. There is so much wisdom in this request. I personally believe that what they were really asking was that Jesus would teach them how to pray *to get results.* After all, what would be the point of praying if we would not receive what we were praying for? As I said in an earlier chapter, not receiving what I desired when I prayed was very discouraging for me. It made me want to stop praying, or at least question what was wrong. As Jesus begins to give them a guide to prayer, he gave them the answer to their desire in the first statement. Here, he says when you pray to the Father, simply ask that His will be done. That whatever is happening in heaven be manifested in the earth; this is the will of God.

It is amazing to me how many born again, spirit-filled, bible reading Christians don't know the will of God. It seems as if they are afraid to ask for His will in situations where His will is not clearly obvious. This is why we need to allow the Holy Spirit to pray through us. He knows the mind of God. Romans 8:27 (NKJV) makes this clear, *"Now He who searches the hearts knows what the mind of the Spirit is, because He makes intercession for the saints according to the will of God."* When you know the mind of God, you can pray what God is thinking.

Isaiah Chapter 11 speaks of a Kingdom of Peace. It speaks of the stump of David's family that will grow a shoot (The Messiah)bearing fruit from the old root. Verse 2 of that chapter reads like this: *"The Spirit of the LORD shall rest upon Him, The Spirit of wisdom and understanding, The Spirit of counsel and might, The Spirit of knowledge and of the fear of the LORD."* Now, you may be wondering what this scripture has to do with prayer? It has everything to do with Spirit-led prayer. It has everything to do with praying the will of the Father. When Jesus told his disciples that greater works would they do than what he did, this could only be accomplished through the power of Holy Spirit. When Holy Spirit rests upon you during prayer, when He stirs you to pray, He releases what is needed at that time. He releases in you and out of you what needs to be prayed for that situation. The Spirit of wisdom and understanding reside in every spirit-filled believer. Many times, this wisdom and understanding is beyond our present knowledge or experience. And yet, because Holy Spirit knows the mind of God, He will go beyond our natural ability and pull from our supernatural container to express the will of God in prayer.

I have often been amazed at the words I hear coming out of my mouth during my prayer time. Yet, I know that I am praying the will of God, because of the peace that comes with it. When the Spirit of the Lord rests upon you, you can literally feel his presence. This is why it is so important that when you enter into your prayer time that you do not begin speaking immediately. Start off listening as you bask in the presence of the Lord. Give Holy Spirit an opportunity to deliver the message from heaven that needs to be prayed for that moment. When we fail to do this, we will often pray what we want rather than what God's will is. We also run the risk of not getting our prayers answered according to James 4:3, *"You ask [God for something] and do not receive it, because you ask with wrong motives [out of selfishness or with an unrighteous agenda], so that [when you get what you want] you may spend it on your [hedonistic] desires."*

Another reason to wait on Holy Spirit to reveal what should be prayed is because of the Spirit of counsel and might. I have been in prayer times when I did not want to pray what God wanted me to pray about a situation or a person. During those times, I would have to take some time to allow Holy Spirit to counsel me on why it was better to allow the will of God to be done. He would counsel me with

Scriptures and comforting words. Sometimes, if I needed more prodding, He would convict me for my rebellious nature. Holy Spirit is very good about presenting evidence in the Word of God to remind you what to do with your natural mind:

...casting down arguments and every high thing that exalts itself against the knowledge of God, bringing every thought into captivity to the obedience of Christ.
(2 Corinthians 10:5 NKJV)

When I would eventually yield, the Spirit of might would come upon me to pray the will of God despite how I may have felt about it. It was the Spirit of knowledge (what I knew about God) and the Spirit of the fear of the Lord (my reverence for Him) that eventually led me to victory in my prayer life.

Spirit-led prayers are prophetic prayers, they say what God is saying. Jesus said in John 12:49 (NLT), *"I don't speak on my own authority. The Father who sent me has commanded me what to say and how to say it."* The results of prophetic prayers manifest themselves in supernatural ways. Powers in the natural realm have no dominion over the supernatural power of prophetic prayers. Prophetic prayers are fueled by faith. Faith operates in the unseen realm to bring manifestation into the earth realm. Hebrews 11:1 states, *"Now faith is the substance of things hoped for, the evidence of things not seen."* The words you speak by faith are creative words. When you repeat words in prayer that have come from the mouth of God, you can expect to see what you said! You can expect the will of God to be seen in the earth as it is in heaven!

In the bible, we read where many of God's prophets would pray and they would receive what they prayed for.

Surely the Lord GOD does nothing, Unless He reveals His secret to His servants the prophets."
(Amos 3:7 NKJV)

The true prophets of God were the voice of God in the earth. So, quite naturally, whatever they said would be manifested in the earth. But what about those who are not called to be a prophet? Did you know that you can still pray the mind of God? That you can still speak what God's will is and see it come to pass? I believe this is what happened with the woman with the issue of blood.

And suddenly, a woman who had a flow of blood for twelve years came from behind and touched the hem of His garment. For she said to herself, "If only I may touch His garment, I shall be made well."
(Matthew 9:20-21)

I sincerely believe that what this woman said to herself was what God was saying about her. I believe that she was speaking what the will of God was for her life. Look at what the rest of the story says:

But Jesus turned around, and when He saw her He said, "Be of good cheer, daughter; your faith has made you well." And the woman was made well from that hour.
(Matthew 9:22)

This was a supernatural manifestation of faith coupled with prayer. What did not happen for her for 12 years in the natural, happened for her immediately in the supernatural! I believe the Spirit of the Lord rested upon her and the Spirit of Wisdom directed her to her healing place. The counsel of man told her to stay home, but the Spirit of might came upon her and she did the unusual and she received supernatural healing

I want to close this chapter by encouraging you to read your bible daily. Become intimately acquainted with the God of the bible and see how he works in the lives of his people. Memorize the Scriptures, so that when you pray you will pray God's word. The more Word you plant in your spirit man, the more effectively the Holy Spirit can pray through you? Nothing makes prayer easier than praying what God has already said. Nothing makes prayer more victorious than speaking the word of God to the enemy and watching him flee.

Spend more time with Holy Spirit. He will open up your understanding. He will empower you to pray effectively. Prayer time will become your favorite time. You will learn how to develop a praying spirit that never stops praying, even while you are sleeping. 1 Thessalonians 5:17

will become your lifestyle - *pray without ceasing.* Spirit-led prayers get results!

Chapter 6

The Key to It All

But seek first the kingdom of God and His righteousness,
and all these things shall be added to you.
Matthew 6:33 (NKJV)

I remember once listening to a Success Coach who promised to give you the keys to success no matter what "thing" you were into. She went on to say that oftentimes we attend seminars that offer the same promise. However, we tend to walk away with more products, information overload, time lost, and more money spent and not receiving what you paid to receive or what was promised. That is what my prayer journey felt like for many, many years. Most seasoned saints would not make that confession, but I cannot help you by hiding the truth from you. I don't have a monopoly on how to get prayers answered. I want to share what I have learned with everyone I can, because the revelation came from the Holy

Spirit, and now I have a responsibility to share it with the Body of Christ.

Matthew 6:33 is one of the bible verses Christians like to recite because of the statement that comes after the comma: *"...and all these things shall be added to you."* The key word in that sentence which really gets our engines revving is "things." Truth be told, we spend much more time praying about things than we do about seeking the kingdom of God and His righteousness. While no one really wants to admit it, or maybe didn't recognize it, this is one of the biggest roadblocks to getting a prayer answered other than sin.

The last ten verses in Matthew Chapter 6 talk about things and how we should not let them be the central part of our thoughts. Jesus begins this teaching with verse 24: *"No one can serve two masters; for either he will hate the one and love the other, or else he will be loyal to the one and despise the other. You cannot serve God and mammon."* Jesus did not say you *shall not* serve God and mammon. He said you CANNOT. That means it is not possible, even if you have them both. I am certain that Jesus was not teaching against having riches, because scripture teaches us that it is God who gives us the power to obtain wealth (Deuteronomy 8:18). Jesus was trying to get them to understand the wickedness of riches when it is given the central seat of your heart. He was also trying to get them to understand that we serve a jealous God who will not take a backseat to any other god.

Mammon, defined in Webster's 1828 dictionary, is *riches; wealth; or the god of riches.* Hate defined is *to dislike greatly; to have a great aversion to.* The Greek definition of "serve" as it relates to this text means *to be in bondage to.* Are you getting the picture that Jesus is painting? Spirit-led prayers are prayers that are prayed free from the bondage of mammon-related thoughts. Spirit-led prayers are not mammon-driven. Spirit-led prayers are not about things, but about seeking the kingdom of God and his righteousness. Before I received this revelation, I didn't realize how much I actually prayed about things. I did not realize that seeking God was not at the center of my prayer time. I had the fervency and the consistency, but I did not have the results. I thought I was praying like a **warrior** when, in truth, I was praying like a **worrier.**

Don't worry about anything; instead, pray about everything. Tell God what you need, and thank him for all he has done.
(Philippians 4:6 NLT)

I worried about the things I needed like food and clothes, and wants of every kind. And when I did not get what I prayed for, the way I felt towards God was not honorable. Rather than seek Him, I sought after the god of riches to meet my needs. This led to an abundance of debt (bondage), strained relationships on many levels, shame, compromised integrity, and lack. And the worst part was when I realized I could no longer hear God the way I used to. I could not function in the Word the way I desired to. Or I should say, the Word could not function in me the way I desired it to.

Now he who received seed among the thorns is he who hears the word, and the cares of this world and the deceitfulness of riches choke the word, and he becomes unfruitful:
(Matthew 13:22 NKJV)

My prayer life was unfruitful because no man can serve God and mammon!

As shameful as this story is to tell, it does have a good ending: Romans 8:28 (NKJV), *"And we know that all things work together for good to those who love God, to those who are the called according to His purpose."* At the core of my being, I knew that I loved God and, without a doubt, I knew He loved me more. It was during that time that I got to know God in a greater and different dimension. As I stated at the beginning of the book, I only had one perception of God and it was not as a loving Father. Thankfully, that's just what he has now become at this time in my life. He brought me up out of my mess and embraced me. He did not scold me. He did not punish me. He rescued me. With the help of Holy Spirit, my prayer life totally changed. I no longer enter prayer asking for things. Instead, I rest in Matthew 6:32, *"for your heavenly Father knows that you have need of all these things."* It was during this time that I began to learn who my Father God really was and why I no longer needed to worry about anything. Here are just a few of the names I learned:

- Jehovah Tsidkenu, He is my righteousness.
- Jehovah Mekoddishkem, He sanctifies me.
- Jehovah Shalom, He is my peace.
- Jehovah Shammah, He is present with me.
- Jehovah Rophe, He is the God who heals me.
- Jehovah Jireh, He is the Lord who provides for me.
- Jehovah Nissi, He is the Lord my Banner who goes before me in battle.
- Jehovah Rohi, He is the Lord my shepherd.

Every one of these names revealed to me a loving Father who cared about me and had already provided everything I would ever need, even before I knew that I needed it. This revelation in our relationship changed everything about the way I prayed. I realized that the only need I really had was to get to know the Father more and more. The more I knew Him and his heart, the more prayers I began to see answered consistently.

If you abide in Me, and My words abide in you, you will ask what you desire, and it shall be done for you. 8 By this My Father is glorified, that you bear much fruit; so you will be My disciples.
(John 15:7-8)

Glorified means honored, praised, and worshiped. When prayers are answered, it causes one to honor, praise, and worship God. God is pleased when we bear the fruit of answered prayers. He is pleased when we choose to abide in Him, because it pleases him to answer prayers.

The key to praying Spirit-led prayers is abiding in the Father. I would like to tell you that once I got this revelation that all my prayers were answered, all my debt was cleaned up, and all my troubles were over. In reality, this was just the beginning of the journey. The first thing I noticed that happened as I began abiding with him was that I spent a lot of time in tears. I sensed this to be a cleansing of my soul. Had God given me everything that I needed without going through this cleansing process, I would have been no different than the person I was prior to this revelation. I was being engrafted (implanted) into the vine: *"Wherefore lay apart all filthiness and superfluity of naughtiness, and receive with meekness the engrafted word, which is able to save your souls"* (James 1:21 KJV). My soul (mind, will, emotions, intellect) needed to be cleansed. This was not a painful process as much as it was draining. I made up my mind that I wanted help, so the pain was not as obvious. It was draining because Holy Spirit was doing all the work. He was praying for me and I was being set free with every session. Spirit-led prayers get results.

Also I noticed that as our fellowship and relationship grew, my Father invited me to partner with him in getting his will done in the earth. I remember so vividly early one morning as I was kneeling in prayer, I heard him say, "I can trust you with people." These words literally caused me to cry with such humility. I had become one with the heart of the Father. I knew how much he loved his people because of the way he loved me.

The secret of the LORD *is with those who fear Him,*
And He will show them His covenant.

Psalm 25:14 (NKJV)

I was entering a place where Holy Spirit could speak confidentially to me. My level of prayer was escalating. I would begin to pray for others as directed by Holy Spirit and I would see results. Sometimes, there was an enemy that needed to be exposed, a sickness that needed to be healed, or a deliverance that needed to happen. All of these things required someone to stand in the gap to pray for God's will to be released in each situation. Rarely, if ever, would anyone know that God used me to participate in the process. And there were other times when I had no idea who I was praying for. I prayed as Holy Spirit directed. All the glory was for God and Him alone!

Eventually, the time came for me to pray for myself, as Holy Spirit would direct. He was teaching me a whole new way of praying and receiving what I asked for in prayer. One day I was abiding with my Father in my prayer room, not asking for anything. I was just listening. There were some things happening in my life that needed His attention, but He already knew that. As I was resting in Him, I heard Holy Spirit say to me, *"Pray this. Stretch out Your hand over my enemies."* Now, this may seem like nothing special to some, but it was awesome to me. You see, just the week before, Holy Spirit spoke to my heart and said, *"Now is the time to ask."* Now He tells me what to ask for. That is Spirit-led praying!

As Holy Spirit continued to instruct me regarding this prayer, He explained to me what it means when God stretches his hand out over my enemies. He said, *"Your enemies are everything, everybody, every entity, and every force that is blocking your progress to obtaining my promise. When God stretches His hand over your enemies, it is not to bless them, it is to destroy them! It is to bless you."*

Though I walk in the midst of trouble, You will revive me;
You will stretch out Your hand Against the wrath of my
enemies, And Your right hand will save me.
(Psalm 138:7 NKJV)

Holy Spirit did not instruct me to name my enemies. He did not allow my natural mind to participate. It is possible that I would have missed some or named the wrong thing. It is possible that those enemies that were hidden would have remained untouched, because I would not know to call them out. God knows all things, and I was giving him permission to destroy all of my enemies. I was partnering with him so that whatever His will was in heaven, would be done in the earth in my life.

He began to give me new prayer strategies and open my mind up to things that I had not thought about. One night as I was sitting in a service at a church I was visiting,

53

during worship, I heard Holy Spirit say to me again, *"Pray this. Close the portals of the second heavens. Close the portal of the kingdom of darkness that is open over you."*

For we do not wrestle against flesh and blood, but against principalities, against powers, against the rulers of the darkness of this age, against spiritual hosts of wickedness in the heavenly places.
(Ephesians 6:12 NKJV)

He then said, *"Ask this. Open the windows of heaven and pour out Your blessings upon me."*

Ask of Me, and I will give You The nations for Your inheritance, And the ends of the earth for Your possession.
(Psalm 2:8 NKJV)

Once again, this is Spirit-led praying. Since I have been praying this way, and as the Holy Spirit gives me what to say, I have experienced amazingly quick answers to prayer. This has been a most exciting journey and I am blessed to be in partnership with the Kingdom of God to pray the will of God into the earth as it is in heaven.

I close with the final thing that Holy Spirit has taught me about Spirit-led prayers. I used to think if I prayed the right prayers, everything I needed would just magically fall from the sky. I thought things would appear out of nowhere. One day, as I was driving and thinking these thoughts, Holy

Spirit said to me, "Things don't fall out of the sky. They don't drop out of heaven. What does come from Heaven is a word from God. That word is the way to get the things you need. It will lead you to the person, place, or thing that you are believing for.

> *Trust in the LORD with all your heart; do not depend on*
> *your own understanding. Seek his will in all you do, and*
> *he will show you which path to take.*
> (Proverbs 3:5-6 NLT)

The money won't fall out of the sky to pay off that debt, but God will give you the wisdom and the plan. That house will not drop out of the sky, but God will direct you to where it is or to the person who can lead you there. Whatever you need is not just going to fall out of heaven. It is not the way God normally works to get our needs met. We have the Holy Spirit abiding on the inside of us. He will lead and guide you into all truth.

> *Your ears shall hear a word behind you, saying,*
> *"This is the way, walk in it," Whenever you turn to the*
> *right hand or whenever you turn to the left.*
> (Isaiah 30:21 NKJV)

Learning to live this way, pray this way, and walk this way is a process. I am still learning with each experience. If you are like me, it will take time to unlearn or break the habit of praying without the leading of the Holy

Spirit. It will take time to trust and rest in God's presence even in the midst of crisis. It will take much work to turn off the natural mind so that you can hear with the mind of the spirit. But it can be done. The more you learn the voice of Holy Spirit, the easier it will be to follow His leading. And the more you receive answers to your prayers, the more enjoyable your prayer life will become. Spirit-led prayers get results!

Prayer

Heavenly Father, in the Name of Jesus, I pray for every person who has read this book. I pray that the eyes of their understanding have been enlightened, and that the words that they have received have been embedded into the good ground of their hearts. I pray that Holy Spirit is drawing them to the secret place of prayer to experience the peaceful, powerful presence of God.

I pray that every demonic portal in the kingdom of darkness that has an assignment targeted to distract, disrupt, or destroy their prayer life be demolished now in the Name of Jesus! I ask you, Father God, to assign warring angels now that will close every satanic portal and cause it to be powerless, ineffective, and fruitless in the prayer lives of your people.

Heavenly Father, now open every portal in the Kingdom of heaven and pour out your dynamic power in the prayer lives of these readers. Holy Spirit, speak clearly to each and every one of them as they sit quietly in the presence of God. May the cleansing power of the efficacious blood of Jesus be applied to every heart in preparation to pray according to the will of God.

Father, I thank you for the fruit of supernatural and accelerated answers to prayers in their lives from this day forward.

In Jesus' Name, I pray. Amen.

About the Author

Karen Jethroe

is a spiritually gifted communicator who sagaciously applies biblical truths to present day situations. A sound and seasoned, well-respected writer, speaker, conference host, mentor, friend and pastor, her call and passion is to empower women to live the life that God has created them to live.

Up From the Ashes Women's Ministry is the vehicle that she uses to educate, enlighten, and embolden women of all ages and from all walks of life. The rhetoric that she uses is anointed, engaging, revelatory, and challenging. As she freely shares personal stories about her own steps to freedom, many women have been catapulted to experience the same liberty in their own lives.

Up From the Ashes Women's Ministry is for every woman, every church, and every community where there are women who are looking for the impetus to rise above the ashes of their past and permission to run their race with passion, purpose and precision.

Karen Jethroe serves as Senior Pastor of Kingdom Life Christian Ministries in Belleville, IL, Founder of Up From the Ashes Women's Ministry, Overseer for Deliverance Church in Malawi, South Africa and Owner of Kingdom Purpose Productions, LLC.

She enjoys life with her husband Dennis, their four adult children, and their 11 grandchildren.

She has an earned Bachelor's Degree in Organizational Leadership from Greenville College and a Master's Degree in Communication from Lindenwood University.

For more information please visit
www.karenjethroe.com

Made in the USA
Lexington, KY
16 August 2018